The *Joy of* Being a Bereavement Minister

The
Joy of
Being a
Bereavement
Minister

Nancy T. Stout

Resurrection Press
An Imprint of
CATHOLIC BOOK PUBLISHING CORP.
Totowa • New Jersey

First published in March, 2005 by

Catholic Book Publishing/Resurrection Press
77 West End Road
Totowa, NJ 07512

ISBN 1-878718-90-8

Library of Congress Catalog Number: 2004117495

Scripture quotations are from the New Revised Standard Version of the Bible, copyright 1989 by the Division of Christian Education of the National Council of the Churches of Christ in the USA. Used by per-mission. All rights reserved.

Cover design by Beth DeNapoli

Printed in the United States of America.

1 2 3 4 5 6 7 8 9

www.catholicbookpublishing.com

DEDICATION

To the families we serve at St. Elizabeth's, for the privilege of sharing your grief journey and in memory of your loved ones.

ACKNOWLEDGMENTS

With much love to Tom and Chris, my "cheerleaders" and to Karen, my "special assistant."

Special thanks to the dedicated volunteers who joined in my vision for this ministry.

In gratitude to Father Dillingham for his support.

With affection to Father Jay for "planting" this book idea in me, and for your guidance, encouragement, and friendship.

Contents

Foreword

As the Church enters a third millennium, many faith communities are still far from taking full advantage of the pastoral resources present in the parish to meet the pastoral needs of parishioners. This carefully crafted and deeply reflective book makes a welcome contribution to those of us who feel the call to serve our communities through ministries of care.

The book can be read at multiple levels of interest— practical, theological, and contemplative. Any of these levels alone would make it well worth reading. All of them together make it a must-read for bereavement ministers and an advisable read for pastoral ministers of all kinds.

At one level, this book can serve as a practical guide for lay ministry empowerment, a concise "how-to" manual, dealing with such fundamental matters as effective recruitment of volunteers, shared visioning, ministry planning, commitment, training and formation, leadership style, ministerial self care, accountability, and support.

At a second and deeper level, the book can be read as a theological reflection on the ministry to the bereaved in particular, or on pastoral ministry in general.

At this level, the author places an outreach ministry to the grieving in its historical and ecclesiastical context. The theological meaning and import of the ministry is traced back to the Old Testament and up through the Vatican II documents.

In particular, the book repeatedly underscores the counter-cultural value of Christian community and the way a Christian ministry to the bereaved helps to heal a culture that denies death, ignores or minimizes pain and suffering, and values individual fulfillment over corporate well-being.

At its deepest level, the book can be read as a reflection upon the spiritual underpinnings of a Christian bereavement ministry. A sense of paradox serves as a prerequisite for understanding this level of the book's meaning. The very title points to the seeming contradiction of a ministry to people in a season of pain and grief that can somehow become joy-full and deeply rewarding. This kind of paradox lies at the core of the Paschal Mystery and of the spiritual life in general.

Given the courage and level of risk to which bereavement ministers are routinely exposed, there are few who would be drawn to such a ministry for ego reasons alone. Yet, becoming a "wounded healer" (another paradox) in service to the bereaved may open one to a deeper level of understanding that can result in the freedom and joy promised by Jesus to those who would find their lives by losing them.

The author's definition of bereavement ministry as "the act of being *present* with someone who is grieving the loss of a loved one" points to the contemplative nature of all truly Christian ministry. To notice, to pay attention, to be present—these are hallmarks of a contemplative approach to life and ministry.

Even a cursory reading of the gospels reveals the extraordinary presence that must have characterized the ministry of Jesus himself. A ministry that is not rooted in and does not flow naturally from a deeply contemplative stance and a lived experience of God's love may be helpful but will not represent the full flowering of Christian ministry.

Reading this book is like sitting with someone who is a personal effectiveness coach, experienced mentor, pastoral theologian and spiritual companion all rolled into one. I encourage you to answer the questions for reflection at the end of each chapter. By doing so, you will find yourself engaged in a personal conversation that could change your life. This deceptively small book will lead you to the threshold of your own baptismal vocation to serve God's people.

> John G. Gutting, Ph.D.
> Adjunct Associate Professor of Pastoral Studies
> The Athenaeum of Ohio/Mt. St. Mary's Seminary

Introduction

A re you looking for a resource for your parish bereavement committee? Have you been wondering if God is calling you to minister to the grieving? Do you have questions about exactly what bereavement ministry is? This small book can serve to provide helpful information, stimulate prayerful personal reflection, and facilitate discussion and lay development within your parish community. It is intended to be a resource for laity and clergy who are already engaged in bereavement work or who are exploring the possibilities for individual ministry and/or ministry in a parish.

Bereavement ministry is becoming more prominent within the life of parish communities today as we deepen our awareness and understanding of the Christian call to comfort the grieving among us. The pastoral basis is firmly rooted in Christian theology and Holy Scripture, as well as in Church tradition. We find examples and stories of "reaching out" to the bereaved as far back as the Old Testament and certainly in stories of Jesus in the Gospel. We have official instruction about this work in the *Catechism of the Catholic Church* and in Vatican II documents. Learning about this rich background of the ministry helps establish a foundation for parishes and priests who seek to serve.

If you've been doing this work for a while, you know that it is not necessarily one of those "fun" ministries that everyone in the parish is lining up to do. But you also know the reward and satisfaction that comes from being present to a person in times of loss and sadness. It is certainly not for everyone; it can even be a bit intimidating. There must be a true discernment process before entering this ministry. However, the challenge of ministry to the grieving strengthens and deepens one's faith. It nurtures the bond of connection we have with each other as human beings. It teaches about the mystery of God's love for all, especially the suffering, and it shows the model of Jesus in his own ministry.

Bereavement ministry provides an opportunity for personal spiritual growth, and in some instances the ministers receive far more than they give. The sense of community within a parish is enhanced as members learn a new way to "care for" those in need, to offer the gift of Christian love, to experience again the mystery of Jesus Christ alive in our actions and words.

I have truly been gifted these past two years by the generosity of those who joined me to do this work. It has been a privilege to provide leadership and guidance, to share stories and listen to one another, and to join together in prayer. The deeper blessing comes from the powerful witness of the very ones we serve—those grieving the loss of a loved one. Their strength and faith and gracious reception of our contact are all an inspiration as we live out the Christian call to service.

I hope that what I've written here might inspire you as you develop a bereavement ministry in your parish or support what already exists. There is helpful information for getting started, for recruiting volunteers, and for preparing the ministers to go out and to serve. It is a story, in part, of my experience in a parish that needed and was ready for a special ministry to the grieving. It starts at the beginning—with a proposal on paper submitted to the parish staff. The book goes on to describe the step-by-step process of organizing and sustaining our "Lazarus ministry." It includes real stories of the encounters of the volunteers as they interacted with grieving members in our parish. The story is unfinished, of course, as this ministry becomes rooted in the parish. Perhaps with the help of this book, you can begin your own story!

Chapter 1

Touching Others' Pain

BEREAVEMENT ministry can be defined as the act of being present with someone who is grieving the loss of a loved one. It happens within the context of faith, and, in this context, is a caring, supportive, and compassionate ministry on the part of one parishioner for another.

Let's look at these adjectives for a moment. Compassion—"*com passio*"—means "with feeling," to "suffer with." An act of compassion draws one into the inner feelings of another who is suffering . . . consequently, the pain and sadness are shared by both. The ministers are called to comfort and to support. Bereavement ministry does not involve taking away the pain of the grieving person. Rather it is journeying in that pain with the one who is grieving.

We are all familiar with the gestures associated with expressing sympathy at the time of a death or loss. The act of sympathizing usually involves something immediate such as sending a flower arrangement, writing a card, visiting at the wake, and/or attending the funeral liturgy. Often our expression of sympathy ends right there; it tends to be short term.

All of these gestures are very appropriate and mean much to the grieving relatives of the deceased. And these same gestures can certainly be incorporated into any bereavement ministry. But ministry . . . ministering to others . . . serving . . . can go well beyond these gestures.

It involves being present more deeply, more completely, and for the longer term. Ministry asks for an entering into the feelings of sadness and loss in a more personal way. And, finally, it requires exposing oneself, if you will, to the more "raw" feelings of anguish that might not be shown in public. Herein is the risk in serving in this ministry. One commits to being present, to following through, and to "walking with" the bereaved through some unknown and possibly unfamiliar emotional territory. Everyone's grief is personal and unique, and it can be unpredictable—a true roller coaster of emotions, memories, even regrets. The bereavement minister agrees to ride that roller coaster with the one who is grieving.

Consider a woman who has experienced a series of significant losses—the deaths of three loved ones in less than a year's time. She is in the midst of a very complicated grief journey. Her pain is raw; the tears and the deep feelings of sadness and confusion and anger are right on the surface and seemingly "uncontrollable" to the woman. It takes courage for the bereavement minister to approach the bereaved initially. And then it takes great patience and sensitivity for the minister to hear this woman's story. Yet this is the call of the ministry.

Dr. Elizabeth Kubler-Ross worked with dying populations in various settings for many years, and she studied the process that unfolds with the "letting go" of dying. She observed that the dying and their loved ones went through these common stages: shock and denial, anger and rage, grief and pain, and finally peace and acceptance. At first glance, the stages are presented as a neat and tidy process. There are steps to go through; one leads to the next until the end comes . . . that of peace and acceptance of the loss. Would that it were so! The minister's work would be so simple and so much less intense, to say nothing of the bereaved's experience!

While these stages of grief are quite legitimate and descriptive of the grief journey, it is rarely a straight line from point A to point B. The grief journey twists and turns and doubles back on itself. The grieving person passes through anger and denial to bargaining, and just when acceptance appears within reach, the anger rises up again and takes over—surprising and maybe even shocking. Stages, yes, but a predictable order? A timeline for resolving the pain of grief and loss? Not very likely in my personal and professional experience.

So the bereavement minister comes into the process to offer aid and care and to attend to the person in pain. The minister wishes to contribute to the eventual comfort and happiness of those who grieve; the minister steps on the pathway with them and offers a gift—the hope of the resurrection. This gift is at the center of bereavement work as a parish lay ministry.

From Darkness to Hope

In a beautiful story in John's Gospel, Chapter 11:1-44, we read of the friendship between Jesus and Lazarus and his sisters, Mary and Martha. This relationship is mentioned and described in other Gospel passages, as well, and in each of these the Scripture indicates that they knew each other well and spent time in one another's company. We too know and understand the bonds of friendship in our lives, and we can relate to these biblical stories.

Jesus hears of Lazarus' illness and death. When Martha comes to meet him with the news, his first instinct is to offer comfort to her, to minister to her in her grief. Here is the model for bereavement ministry—for Lazarus Ministries in parishes today. The Lord reaches out to Martha who is grieving the loss of her brother. The hope he offers and holds out before her is exactly that which we offer to those we serve today. It is the promise and the hope of the resurrection after death. Jesus tells Martha that there is more than death and that there is something beyond the darkness of the loss. And in response, Martha declares her belief and her recognition of Jesus as the Christ.

This encounter illustrates the first dimension of the Gospel story that impacts our ministry today. Although we cannot take away the suffering of the bereaved; we can listen and offer quiet presence and support. We can provide a safe setting in which the grieving can express their painful feelings and be a source of encouragement as they move forward in the letting go process. And always the gift we have to keep in front of them is exactly this hope of and belief in the resurrection. Death is not the end. We hear that from Jesus himself.

The second dimension of this story is the reaction Jesus had to his friend's death. Scripture says Jesus was "greatly disturbed in spirit and deeply moved." Jesus, the Lord Himself, the one who is the resurrection and the life for us, grieved at the death of his friend. Like us in all things, Jesus felt the pain of death, of loss and separation, brief as it was. He wept at the tomb so that others could say, "See how he loved him."

So Jesus models the normal feelings of grief at the death of his beloved friend. It is this grief that the bereavement ministry addresses. Christian communities gather around those who are grieving, and they follow through on their desire to alleviate the suffering they see in their midst. The ministers communicate the presence of God to the bereaved. They model the love of one's neighbor in the name of the parish and Christian community and, most importantly, in the name of Jesus, the one who loved most purely and completely.

"Wounded Healers"

Any involvement in ministry to the grieving commands a personal understanding of loss and grief, of the dynamics at work in suffering, and even some knowledge of the Christian theology of death and suffering. The bereavement minister approaches the grieving out of his/her personal experience of previous losses in life. In a ministry this intense and intimate, it is inevitable that memories are triggered and that questions regarding faith might surface. So those who look at involvement in the ministry need to pay attention first to their personal history with grief issues and to resolution of these issues.

Yet it seems to be just these folks who have known loss and grief in their own lives who are the most drawn to working with others in the grieving process. What could be more poignant than a woman who experienced the devastating pain of her own child's death now reaching out and listening to the parents of a young woman killed in a car accident? Under the proper conditions, the personal histories and experiences of the ministers lend themselves to the support and empathy for the bereaved seeking counsel, rather than detracting from them

The elderly man whose wife of 60+ years has died looks to the minister for comfort and assurance that he'll make it on his own now. He wants an attentive ear as he recalls the beloved whose life he shared. The effective bereavement minister will maintain just enough "distance" to hear the widower's concerns and fears. The minister may bond by sharing a personal story or experience, but he/she will not get caught up in his/her own feelings so that the focus shifts away from the bereaved. Balance in this special relationship is quite important.

Also, it bears consideration that the pain you may touch as a bereavement minister can be other than sadness at a death. It can be regret over missed opportunities. It can be anger at old wounds and hurts and conflicts from the past. It can be jealousy; it can be shame at feeling relieved about the death. There are all sorts of scenarios the bereavement ministry volunteer can walk into. Perhaps this is why the bereaved are sometimes regarded as "untouchables" in our culture; people around them are afraid of the pain and sorrow they see, and, oddly enough, are almost afraid that such "bad luck" may actually be catching! For example, a widow might be uncomfortable going out with her best friend and husband because it used to be an activity for the two couples, and now the widow is just a "third wheel."

The Gift of Kinship

Bereavement ministers do make a sacrifice for this ministry. They sacrifice personal time and energy and emotion. They risk exposure to unpleasant feelings and even uncomfortable situations. They risk being touched in their very souls by encountering the vulnerabilities of the bereaved. But they also risk being "gifted" by those who are grieving. And this risk the volunteers have willingly—even enthusiastically—embraced.

It is a certainty that every member of a bereavement ministry committee will, at some time, experience his/her own painful loss or death of a loved one. It is one element that makes this ministry and those who serve in it quite unique. Death and loss and the accompanying feelings are universal. Also, any parish today will be touched as a community by many losses over time; the parish members will often share in the sadness of grief at a particular loss. And always, as Christians, we hold fast to the heart of the mystery of our professed faith—the hope of the resurrection and of eternal life with our God.

Again, we look to our model, Jesus. He met many in his ministry who had experienced loss of all kinds, including daughters, brothers, and other loved ones. He showed compassion and grieved with them. As Matthew 14:14 reads, "He had compassion for them and cured their sick." Jesus also had his own farewells in his short life. He knew firsthand what loss and sorrow was; he knew the powerful emotions it can evoke in us, and he experienced these fully with us. Different translations of the raising of Lazarus describe Jesus as "greatly disturbed," "deeply moved," "perturbed" and "sighing again." Deep and sincere empathy and "feeling with". . . this is what those serving in the bereavement ministry strive to emulate. There is no doubt that it is a humbling challenge for the ministers.

The bereavement ministry is about kinship; that is, offering the gift of ourselves to each other. Actually it is letting God be in kinship with those who are grieving through our very presence with them. Here I am speaking of the kind of kinship we see Jesus offer from the cross when he bestows his mother Mary and his beloved disciple John into each other's care. Today, Jesus lovingly bestows all of us in that same way into each other's care, particularly in a parish community.

Author Joyce Rupp, OSM writes in her popular book on grieving *Praying Our Goodbyes,* "God reaches into our ache and comforts us by giving us to each other in kinship. . . . kinship is this gift of one to the other." It's a big call; it's a significant commitment to make. The minister may become tired and impatient as time passes, even a little bored with particular situations, but the call is to be faithful to the commitment. Later in the book, Rupp writes, ". . . we can draw energy from one another in our time of need and return it just as generously when the time is called forth."

The Gospel messages call us quite simply to love without expecting anything in return. This is never more clearly illustrated than in the serving ministries in parishes, such as the bereavement ministry. In

2 Corinthians 1:3-5 we read, "Blessed be the God and Father of our Lord Jesus Christ, the Father of mercies and the God of all consolation, who consoles us in all our affliction, so that we may be able to console those who are in any affliction with the consolation with which we ourselves are consoled by God. . . . our consolation is abundant through Christ." In other words, Christian love passing from one to another, looking for and seeing the Christ in one another, and ultimately being Christ for each other is what the bereavement ministry is all about. Touching each other's pain in order to bring comfort and hope and, finally, healing is at the core of this ministry to the grieving.

QUESTIONS FOR REFLECTION/DISCUSSION

1. How is Jesus in the Gospel stories reflected as a model for bereavement ministry?

2. Reflect on a personal experience of receiving "compassion" during a time of loss.

3. What does it feel like to reveal your own vulnerability?

Chapter 2

Care for the Orphans and Widows

Call to Ministry

THE concept of bereavement ministry, of serving the needs of those who are grieving losses, is certainly not a new concept, although it does seem recently that more parishes are developing this particular ministry and naming it as a parish organization. However, the call to serve the grieving is heard even in Old and New Testament Scripture. Church leadership addresses the same call in such official documents as the *Catechism of the Catholic Church* and in the Vatican II document "Decree on the Apostolate of Lay People."

These scriptural "calls" and official "pronouncements" of the Church serve not as a means of justifying bereavement work as a ministry but as a means of supporting and affirming such work as the responsibility of a parish community to its members. In the name of Jesus and of his Church we serve one another.

Beginning with the first chapter of Isaiah, the prophet reports his first oracle of the Lord in verse 17

". . . Learn to do good; seek justice, rescue the oppressed, defend the orphan, plead for the widow."

This call to serve the needs of the marginalized populations remains with us today. The dying, the mentally ill, the elderly, the imprisoned and the grieving are all populations who suffer deeply, who have special needs, and who are sometimes "shunned" by society and hurt by prejudice. Those of us who are able (physically, emotionally, financially) are obligated to help those who are less able at a given time.

This call becomes more specific and firm in the New Testament Letter of James. In Chapter 1, verse 27 we read, "Religion that is pure and undefiled before God, the Father, is this: to care for orphans and widows in their distress and to keep oneself unstained by the world." Some scholars consider this verse to be a practical application of verse 22 in the same chapter, "be doers of the word and not merely hearers." In other words, verse 27 presents some direction about what it is we are to "do" with the word we hear from God. The early Jewish community looked to its leaders for guidelines about life that adhered not only to Hebrew law but also to the "new" law of Jesus' own teachings. The words in the Letter of James set forth just such appropriate guidelines.

Throughout the four Gospels in New Testament Scripture we read the stories about Jesus reaching out to the suffering, to those in need, to disenfranchised populations. There are few direct references to ministry to the bereaved. The most obvious is the story of the raising of Lazarus and Jesus' interaction with Martha and Mary and their community (see pages 20-21).

The story in Luke 7:11-17 is also worth mentioning here. It tells of Jesus responding to the grieving widow who now mourns her only son. Scripture says Jesus "had compassion for her" and said to the widow "Do not weep." It is this compassionate presence that was always a part of Jesus' ministry. Jesus is the embodiment of love; he did not have any formal commissioning to do his work. He modeled the love of God in the world, ministering even to "the least of these." Today we acknowledge the call to "go and do likewise" as we reach out to the bereaved in our parishes.

To hear the Word of God—to really let it into our heart-space—compels us to respond to this word with concrete action. In the Scripture cited above, this means looking out for those less fortunate who might need protection. It is acting in response to the love God shows us each day and letting this love take root and spring forth by sharing it with others in concrete and measurable ways. As Christians today, we are called to live out our faith by being disciples of Jesus. In our faith and spiritual development, we are constantly seeking new and creative understandings of what this means. It can manifest itself in many ways. Each of us discovers our particular gifts, and then we search for the means by which to use them in order to meet the needs of others around us. We have a strong and solid theological basis, a true foundation in our faith, on which to build this parish ministry to the bereaved in our communities.

Parish-based ministries serve in a personal and intentional way. There is structure and support and a network of resources that target a particular need within a community. Bereavement ministry, as any ministry in a parish, begins with a vision and a proposal based upon this perceived need. It is not just a random desire to "do something." It arises from recognition that there are those in our midst who are suffering, and that we share some responsibility in alleviating that suffering. This is who we are as Christians; this is what we do as parish community and as Church.

Faithful Response to the Challenge

This foundation for ministry is further affirmed by these words: "They devoted themselves to the apostles' teaching and fellowship, to the breaking of bread and to the prayers" (Acts 2:42). This scripture passage is an illustration of what parish life today is all about. It is this "communal life" in which we care for one another and build up one another's spirit and commitment to faith. These words describe what it is to be Church; together we experience liturgy, study Scripture and Church teaching, celebrate Eucharist, and pray for and with each other. Bereavement ministry is just one dimension of acting out this call to communal life. It is helping to hold up those who are weaker, knowing they will in turn do the same out of their own strength on another day.

The Vatican II document "Decree on the Apostolate of Lay People" *(Apostolican Actuositatem)* addresses the participation of the laity within the larger Church and the role of the laity in carrying out the Church's mission within the parish. In a way, it is a "how to be Church" document which guides us as Christian disciples in the world. This document acknowledges that each of us is blessed with particular gifts and talents, and that it is an ongoing process to discover what these are and what it is God asks us to do with them. It provides some guidance on how to share them for the benefit of the community of which we are a part.

"In the church there is diversity of ministry but unity of mission" *(AA2)*. As Church, we share common goals and values even though there are various ways of achieving these goals and of modeling these values. "A life like this calls for continuous exercise of faith, hope and charity" *(AA4)*. We can apply these statements to the work of bereavement ministry. Those who sincerely feel/hear a call to serve the grieving, to alleviate suffering in times of loss, do live out this call to discipleship. We put aside personal likes and dislikes, tendencies toward criticism and judgment, and we pour out our compassion toward those in need in our parish community.

On a practical level, this can often be a true challenge. What happens when we're called to minister to a family whose loved one committed suicide? What happens when the deceased was killed in a traffic accident as the result of alcohol use? What about the family whose loved one died from lung cancer caused by cigarette smoking? And the family grieving the death of a child who contracted AIDS by living a particular lifestyle?

As bereavement ministers, we can easily and often be drawn into whatever family drama surrounds a death. The reality is that we do not only serve the family whose matriarch died in her sleep at age 95 after a long and chaste life. We do hear beautiful and even heroic stories about the deceased whose families we serve. But we may just as often hear the sorrows, the struggles and the faults of the deceased and of the mourners. And then we are called to remember again that our presence is to serve and to attempt to alleviate suffering without any judgment on the circumstances surrounding and contributing to that suffering. A challenge, to be sure—a serious challenge. What we pay attention to here is the person who is in pain and in need, not why and how that pain came about. And we ask the questions: What can we do to alleviate the pain? What resources are available to help meet the needs of the one suffering the loss?

Loving our God calls us to love our neighbor. We live out this love of God in this "agape"—a caring and compassionate concern of Christians for humankind. "That is why mercy to the poor and the sick, and charitable works and works of mutual aid for the alleviation of all kinds of human needs, are held in special honor in the church" *(AA8)*. Again here is foundation for our work as bereavement ministers. If we are bound by our love of and for our God, then that love will be visible in our service to others in need. God is sorrowful when one of His own is in pain; as disciples we are the living flesh and blood presence of God. We are the ones who can sit with another and wipe away the tears and hold the hand and embrace the lonely. We see the face of Christ in each other; we serve that Christ in each other.

Another dimension of this ministry is the responsibility we, the laity, have in our communities to assist the pastors, our leaders, in the mission and outreach of the church. ". . . their action (that is the laity) within the Church communities is so necessary that without it, the apostolate of pastors will frequently be unable to obtain its full effect. . . . Laity should develop the habit of working in the parish in close union with their priests . . ." *(AA10)*. This is a clear call to the laity within a parish to participate fully in the mission of the Church, each according to his/her gifts and abilities. The goal is not to engage in a personal or individual campaign or ministry, but in a ministry on behalf of the pastors, the particular parish, and the universal Church founded by Jesus Christ.

Reaching Out

In any parish community, the pastor, priest or deacon will usually be the first person to have contact with the family members and loved ones of the deceased. This is the one who can initially communicate some of the circumstances surrounding a death, and who can identify for the volunteer minister some of the special needs of the bereaved. As with all parish ministries, information needs to be shared—pastor to committee members and vice versa. It is important to relay back to the pastor an identified need for further involvement and follow up with a family after a funeral. This sharing is what helps to create the communal nature of the ministry. It also can serve to build up one another in ministry by providing support and encouragement for pastor and volunteer ministers alike.

Sometimes the concept of this spiritual, supportive ministry of "presence" can seem a bit vague. There is no list of tasks that can be checked off upon completion. There is nothing "for sale"; there is no specific timeline. It's a bit ambiguous, you might think. For our benefit, there is a discussion and description of these spiritual acts and of this ministry of presence in Article 7, Part VI of the *Catechism of the Catholic Church*. It reads, "Instructing, advising, consoling and comforting are spiritual works of mercy. . . ." And again in the Vatican II decree guidance is provided. "Works of charity and mercy bear a most striking testimony to the Christian life . . . training should enable the faithful to learn from very early childhood how to sympathize with our brothers (and sisters), and to help them generously in need" *(AA31c)*. This is all a part of what we are about as disciples of Jesus Christ.

The broad base of support for this special ministry as a parish outreach is rooted in the Old Testament, in the call of Jesus in the Gospel, in the earliest Christian communities, and in modern Church documents and the Catechism. Each illustration and resource affirms the premise of reaching out to others in times of sorrow and loss. Offering comfort to another is not only a human instinct or a response of human nature, but it is scripturally based, doctrinally based, and formally promoted and supported on all levels of Church hierarchy—from the Vatican, to the individual diocese, to the particular parish and pastor.

QUESTIONS FOR REFLECTION/DISCUSSION

1. Discuss the discernment process or sense of "call" that led you to bereavement ministry.

2. What is your understanding of a ministry of "presence?"

3. Read and review the Vatican II document "Decree on the Apostolate of Lay People."

Chapter 3

Companions on the Way

The Vision Dawns

IT begins with a vision—some recognition of a need for the ministry and an idea about how to meet that need. Without this, there is no point from which to build and from which to move forward in the process leading to the implementation stage—the actual creating of a ministry and carrying out the tasks to serve the bereaved in their time of need. But it doesn't stop there. This vision needs to be concretized in words and through discussion, in order for it to become more than just a vision or a "good idea" which can fall to the side along with so many other "good ideas."

In my parish, St. Elizabeth's in Wilmington, Delaware, the first step was my observation of the sheer volume of deaths and funerals taking place in the church and the recognition that there was no structured bereavement program in place. St. Elizabeth's is a city church of approximately 1,600 registered families. They are primarily working class people, many of whom have been members of the parish for two or three generations. The parish has a long-standing relationship with the Benedictine Sisters, who have been associated with the parish school for nearly one hundred years. The majority of funerals in the parish are members or persons with a close association with the parish and/or its school. In the calendar year 2002, when I joined St. E's, there were 84 funerals presided over by our parish priests.

In developing my idea to initiate such a program of ministry, I brought with me both my background and education in parish and pastoral ministry, my knowledge of my personal gifts and capabilities, and my sense of "call" to engage in this work. Typically in parishes today the priests are quite aware of the strengths and shortcomings of their parish communities and of the particular needs of the parish members. However, the priests alone cannot carry out all the ministries and meet all the needs of the parishioners, nor should these be the expectations the parish has of its priests. As disciples in the modern day church, we are all called to step forward and to offer to assist in expanding established ministries and developing new ministries in the parish setting.

The Vision Forms

With all of this in mind, I presented to the priests a simple description of specific tasks a bereavement committee might do to enhance the degree of support and comfort offered to members who lost loved ones.

At St. Elizabeth's, initial ministry to the bereaved was in place. Pastoral presence and involvement at the time of death and preparation for prayerful and meaningful funeral liturgies has been ongoing there for years. The focus of my proposal for bereavement ministry in this particular parish would be follow up care and support and prayerful presence for the grieving, perhaps stretching over the span of a year after a death.

This type of ministry can, of course, take on many different dimensions in a parish depending on the needs and wishes of members. It can include assistance with planning liturgy, presence at the wake and funeral, meal provision for grieving families, housesitting and childcare during funerals, and many other things. The vision we developed for St. E's was for long-term presence and follow up, a "companioning" of the bereaved for an entire calendar year following a death. In discussion, the priests agreed with me that the weeks and months following a death is a time when support often falls away as everyone gets on with their lives. The grieving are often just beginning to get in touch with their feelings of sadness, anger, and loneliness during this same time.

Taking the First Step

After a resounding vote of approval from the priests for my proposal, the next step, as it usually is for parish ministries, was to recruit volunteers—members to serve on a bereavement committee who would share the vision for the parish. We all know that no matter how "good" a proposed idea is and no matter how great the need in the parish may be, nothing will happen and no ministry can take place, without members stepping forward to volunteer to participate in the ministry. It's all about willing and able "bodies" in a parish community. So the call goes out announcing a new parish ministry and requesting assistance, and this recruiting of volunteers can happen in various ways.

At St. E's the recruiting was done by personal invitation to targeted parishioners deemed appropriate by the priests and other leaders for this work and also through a general invitation in the weekly parish bulletin. It happened by telephone calls to people inviting them to join this new work in the parish. I was amazed at the response. Here I was a relative newcomer to the area and to the parish, inviting these men and women to join me in making this proposal a reality. But sometimes all it takes is a personal invitation to come forward. People genuinely want to help; they just don't always know how or where to do it. When the Holy Spirit begins to move in people, though, amazing things can result.

The Vision Materializes

I can still remember our initial meeting as a committee one Sunday after Mass. It was a gathering of a dozen or so parishioners; many were strangers to each other and all of them were new faces to me. We began this venture by introducing ourselves and by sharing a small piece of our personal journeys and what prompted each of us to accept the invitation to the meeting. I presented a simple outline of my proposal for the ministry, and I explained what bereavement support might be at St. Elizabeth Church. Of course, I encouraged comments and suggestions from those attending the meeting. This is especially important in order to build upon a vision, to broaden it and to make it more inclusive in a particular population. The committee members immediately have a sense of participation in the creative process unfolding.

There was a good and positive energy present at this first gathering. There was an excitement about starting this new ministry. People showed a genuine and humble "desire" to serve, and there was recognition of the need in the parish by these parishioners who knew St. E's so well. Many were themselves lifelong members. There was also a willingness to be guided and taught about bereavement ministry. For the most part, the members who attended the initial meeting came seeking a way to serve others out of the blessings and graces they had received in their own times of pain and suffering. Others were looking for a new way to live out their faith in service; they were trying to find their niche in the parish community. To complement all of this, I had a desire, willingness and need to familiarize myself with the personality of this parish community. It was a refreshing time of getting acquainted for all of us, and we discovered among us an openness to God's direction and guidance in our work.

Setting the Tone

I believe the "tone" for the ministry at St. E's was set by this initial sharing, and especially by the courage these parishioners showed in exposing their own pain and loss to me and to each other. Their personal disclosure helped to illustrate the sensitive and fragile nature of this ministry and of those it is designed to serve. In a sense, this very nature of fragility sets it apart from some other lay ministries because it is so clearly a ministry to people who are extremely vulnerable and "exposed"—namely those grieving the loss of a loved one.

So as a group we prayerfully put out some of our stories. I shared my experience with losses—the deaths of my parents and friends, the diagnosis of my Multiple Sclerosis and consequent sacrifice of career, and most recently the challenges of building a new life with my husband in Delaware after living for many years in Ohio. Other volunteers followed suit. A gentleman was grieving the death of his wife several months earlier after a marriage spanning 50+ years. A woman grieved the loss of her son in a tragic accident. Another woman grieved the death of her husband. There was significant loss in the group that gathered.

I could see immediately that these parishioners knew firsthand what pain and loss were. They also knew the benefit of ongoing support during the grieving process; they had experienced this in their own lives.

But there were others in the group who could help to create some balance—those who were in a stronger "place" in their lives. They were seeking new and creative ways to "be Church," specifically in the local parish community, and they wanted to explore the possibility of achieving that in the context of a new parish ministry. There were some folks who expressed their joy at seeing this ministry become a reality because they had long recognized a need in the parish and were "waiting for a leader," as they put it.

Readiness to Serve

There is an extremely important and sensitive issue involved with recruiting and establishing the bereavement committee. In a sense, we are all "wounded healers," to use the late author and priest Henri Nouwen's term. Out of our brokenness some of us are able to direct a deepened compassion, understanding and empathy toward others who are suffering. However, to be effective ministers we need to have an appropriate distance from and integration of our personal pain and loss. If our own grief is too fresh, raw and unprocessed, we will have a difficult time being present to another whose grief is also a new and open, bleeding wound.

Volunteers for this particular work need to be able to step away from their own sorrow to be present with the one served so that the encounter is supportive and strengthening for the bereaved. If the pain of the volunteer overshadows that of the bereaved, effective ministry cannot happen. Supportive ministry is possible only after the volunteer has processed his or her own loss and becomes ready to use the lessons learned in a constructive manner.

Because of this premise, it's advisable that the bereavement committee leader knows some of the story of each volunteer. The leader needs to be familiar with the journey bringing the volunteer to serve in this ministry. The leader can often accommodate to a degree the particular needs and sensitivities of the volunteers. At St. Elizabeth's I found it supportive to pair the volunteers in teams of two whenever possible. All funeral information about the deceased is then shared with a team of two volunteers. This allows them to share the mailings, telephone calls or to alternate taking assignments as they come in. It also provides for a "buddy" to talk to and with whom to share experiences. This is a big "plus" because we know that death, dying, loss and grief are still not popular topics of conversation for most folks.

A few volunteers on my committee prefer less personal contact with the grieving but still want to be involved from a bit of a distance. These folks deferred to their partners in the telephone calls and visits while taking on themselves the mailings of notes and cards. With this kind of flexibility, the volunteers can work within their specific comfort zone while the bereaved are assured of receiving appropriate contact and support along their journey. Again, providing care and support for the volunteers enables them to be more effective ministers to those in need.

Preparation to "Go Out"

Most of us don't need specific "training" to be kind and supportive of someone who is hurting. It seems to be a basic instinct of human nature to offer sympathy to another, whether it's in the form of verbal and written condolences or a quick hug or touch on the shoulder. And there are some people who have an affinity for "knowing what to say and when to say it."

But serving as a volunteer bereavement minister in a parish community means serving in the name of the parish, and on behalf of the pastor and all the community members. Everything the volunteer does reflects on the parish community and the priests. For this reason, some basic and particular education should be provided for the bereavement volunteers. This ministry committee needs certain "tools" to be able to go out and represent the parish. Good intentions are obviously very important but good ministry requires more than this.

I found a few basic guidelines were appropriate and helpful to the volunteers.

1. Remember you are not a counselor.
2. Be a caring presence.
3. Be a loving listener.
4. Make available supportive resources.
5. Remember *again* you are not a counselor.

Training for this ministry doesn't need to entail hours of "classroom" time, and much depends on the committee members and their specific needs and wishes. But some basic information can be provided with the above guidelines, such as the commonly recognized stages of grief, what is generally accepted as "normal" grieving, how to recognize those "red flags" indicating the bereaved needs professional assistance, and where to go for answers to questions and to find appropriate resources to support the grieving.

What worked at St. Elizabeth's was having a professional grief counselor do a series of one-and-a-half hour presentations to the committee. The sessions allowed for discussion and sharing time, as well, and the volunteers were most appreciative and willing to participate in this enrichment program. After the volunteers ministered for several months, we had a follow up session with the same presenter, and she was able to answer questions and address a few issues which arose from particular situations. One year after beginning the Lazarus Ministry at St. E's, the volunteers were interested in further enrichment education opportunities. Of course, there are many things available, and this is one of our goals for the coming year. The more practiced the volunteers become, the more information they will understand and thus incorporate into their ministry.

There is one point I cannot stress enough times to my committee members, and I still emphasize it when we gather for a meeting. It is this: remember you are not a professional counselor. Stay within the boundaries of the ministry. As volunteer ministers, we are to be a caring presence, a loving listener, and we can make available appropriate professional resource information. Education of the volunteers is ongoing as they become more involved with the bereaved in the parish and as they witness various manifestations of the grieving process. But primarily their role is to be a loving and caring support on behalf of the parish community and to model the compassion of Christ toward those who are suffering. Volunteers in this ministry contribute to the healing process.

If the goal of the ministry is to provide long-term support over the course of the first calendar year, it can be helpful to have a loosely structured timetable to insure that all clients receive a uniform minimum of contacts. It is recognized that some bereaved may need and want more than the minimum, and some will not need or desire even that, but it reflects best on the parish if there is some standard set for the ministry, especially when it is a newly organized ministry. This will prove especially helpful when an initial evaluation of the work is conducted.

At St. Elizabeth's our suggested schedule is set up as follows:

- Telephone calls are made by the committee leader within a week or so after the funeral, accompanied by a card and personal note.

- Contact with the bereaved is made by telephone call and/or mail about one month after the death.

- Contact by telephone call and/or mail happens again at three months after the death, accompanied by a Care Note or similar supportive spiritual literature (see page 77).

- Contact is made after six months and it includes a pamphlet listing some available community resources for grief support.

- Contact is made nine months after the death by telephone call and/or a card in the mail.

- Contact on the first anniversary of the death is a telephone call and a special card and note including a prayer card or some other small token of remembrance. A visit may be offered if the bereaved has been receptive to visits throughout the year. At this time, it is expected that most folks will be "dismissed" or referred to appropriate sources as needed.

Obviously this was never set in stone, but it has served well to provide basic guidelines for the volunteers that can be adjusted according to the needs of the clients. And it is, of course, subject to re-evaluation by the committee.

We also offered a personal visit at the beginning of our contacts with bereaved families, but very few people accepted this. Some volunteers did initiate a meeting for coffee and a chat. And I have shared dinner out with a woman I've gotten to know quite well over the past year. Now as we reach the end of this first calendar year, some volunteers seem reluctant to "let go" of the ones they are serving. We have all become rather protective of these amazing individuals who have shared their loss so bravely with us. But we continue to take on the newly bereaved as funerals occur, and we recognize that people need to and should move on in their journey. Besides that, there is simply no possible way we can keep up with the numbers without letting go of some!

With all the necessary groundwork in place, the next step is for the volunteers to just jump in and get started! Many of the questions cannot be asked until there is some springboard of experience and illustration from which to frame them.

Giving and Receiving

The volunteer ministers will quickly discover both the challenges of this unique ministry and the many graces and blessings that it also bestows on both the one serving and the one served. The stories begin to collect and the relationships begin to develop.

One of the joys for me, as ministry coordinator, is making the initial phone calls and hearing the story of the deceased from the loved one. This first contact can also be a rather formidable task, depending on the circumstances surrounding the death. (It's one of the reasons the committee *likes* me to handle these first contacts).

There is always the unexpected (or the possibility for it). Even with reading the basic information from a funeral sheet and an obituary and getting a "heads up" from the pastor, one cannot be prepared for every nuance of an encounter. I continue to be amazed and, indeed, awed by the depth of sharing that sometimes occurs. Perhaps it is that anonymity that surrounds the telephone call—since most times it is not an acquaintance for me and I'm sure that is an advantage of being a newcomer to the community. But people do share when they're invited to do so.

Stories of a long marriage, anecdotes about a beloved child, memories of an elderly parent—all of these pour forth in the need of the bereaved to communicate something about the life of the deceased. Sometimes it's a description of a lengthy illness preceding the death, or maybe it's the suddenness of the loss. "It's a blessing." "It's a relief." "It happened so fast. I can't believe it." "My faith will get me though this." "I don't know what I believe about heaven." I've heard all of these things in the course of my first year of work at St. Elizabeth's.

Rita, a young wife and mother, lost both parents in just the span of a few months. I "met" her (via telephone) shortly after her mom's death, and we immediately felt a particular level of comfort with each other. In particular, she reminded me of myself since I was the same age as Rita when my mother died, and then my dad's death happened the next year. Now, twelve years after those losses in my life, I understood what she felt and what she was experiencing.

Over the course of the next several months, we had many long conversations; I sent cards, notes and pamphlets, other support information, and I recommended books. Rita absorbed everything like a sponge. She was hungry for it all. She truly entered her grief and pain—she felt it all—and she looked for the meaning, for what she could learn, and for how she might deepen her faith through this experience. It was a crisis point for her, a transition, and I was so proud of her courage and her honest grieving.

We both had a sense that God truly blessed our encounters, our connection, and we believed the Holy Spirit was at work in our relationship as I companioned Rita through her grief. Finally we had the opportunity to meet—for real—at St. Elizabeth's All Souls Day Liturgy. We were both deeply touched and moved by our meeting. I saw clearly what bereavement ministry is about, what it can be and what it can mean in the life of one who is grieving and in the life of the bereavement minister. These encounters are *holy;* they are "God-moments." They are precious; they are a sharing of sacred space.

Rita sent me an email that I share with her permission. It says: "Can I just tell you how much I thoroughly enjoyed meeting you several Sundays ago. . . . I feel I am so wise now (still have more growing to do—growth happens every day) in that I see things so much more clearly. . . . All of the time I have spent reflecting has just catapulted me to a new level of self-awareness . . . I had to go through all this to get where I am today. Thank you so much for reaching out to me . . . it has helped me more than you may ever realize."

Not all encounters will be like this one, and they need not be. Also we won't always receive the blessing of knowing how we touched a life. This ministry is not about reaping rewards in the here and now. It is about reaching out in love and compassion to the grieving and sharing the goodness and the power of God's love. We give because we are called to give—we give freely from our hearts.

At St. Elizabeth Church, we draw near to the close of our first year as a parish ministry as I write this. We will close our companioning relationship with many clients as the first anniversary passes for some deaths, and we will celebrate this past year that we have shared as a committee. We have grown as Christians and as disciples in the Church. We have supported one another in this journey with the bereaved of our parish. Some committee members have also marked special anniversary dates of deaths of their own loved ones during this time. They have moved forward in their personal grief journeys and are now able to reach out more completely as others have ministered to them.

This living out of discipleship is always a cycle of giving and receiving—and then giving again. If we truly learn about and experience God's love, we also learn to let ourselves be renewed and re-filled by others, knowing we are always called to give and to pour ourselves out for others, even as Jesus Christ emptied himself for all of us.

QUESTIONS FOR REFECTION/DISCUSSION

1. What obstacles might arise in developing a lay ministry in your parish? And, how is ministry "shared" by priests and laity in your parish?

2. What do you think are the unique characteristics of bereavement ministry?

3. Discuss the basic "tools" you would want/need before serving as a bereavement volunteer.

4. Reflect on the cycle of Christian "giving and receiving."

Chapter 4

Looking Beyond Loss

THIS ministry brings together a group of people in a parish who may know little about each other and who may have little in common with each other. The common ground is the parish to which they belong and in which they serve. The volunteers share a desire to serve the Church by ministering to those who are grieving the loss of a loved one. Often, but not always, the volunteers share some particular significant experience of loss in their own lives which compels them to bring to others what they have learned about loss, grief, and healing.

Bereavement ministry is one heavy with loss and pain—uniquely intense feelings. The volunteers might listen to much sadness, witness many tears, and hear numerous stories of anguish. It can be easy to feel "weighed down" in this ministry or to be subject to early "burn out." It is just these characteristics of bereavement ministry that might scare folks away from offering themselves and their time. There continues to be something mysterious, uncomfortable, and even threatening about death and dying, and around those grieving a death. Perhaps one of the gifts of this type of parish ministry will be to dispel some of the discomfort that surrounds the issue of loss and grief.

So what keeps the volunteers buoyed up? What encourages them, supports them, nurtures them, and refreshes them? The volunteers must receive all of this in order to serve in this deeply emotional work in the parish. They must be able to transcend the pain and distress of loss and move to a deeper level of encountering death and the grief process. It is only in this way that bereavement ministers can discover the true meaning and the joy that is possible in serving those who grieve for a loved one. In this process, they are likely to also move to a deeper level of encountering their own personal faith and trust in God. Confronting any of these big "life" questions leads each of us on an inner search of our soul and a deeper encounter with our God. Any time we are walking with another person and exploring the human condition, the potential for discovery and growth is immense.

What is the source of this joy and meaning? It is most definitely encountered in the hope and the promise of the Passion and Resurrection of Jesus the Christ. All Christians have this help—the abiding knowledge that God suffers with us, that Christ suffered as we do, and that we are not alone and there is much to discover and to explore beyond loss and suffering. Indeed for Christians, Jesus Christ is the bridge that leads us from this loss and suffering to the joy that is freely offered to us. In bereavement ministry, the focus must always be on *life*. Being deeply rooted in a belief in the resurrected Christ and in the hope of eternal life with him provides the foundation of strength needed to participate in bereavement ministry.

Lifting Each Other Up

At. St. E's we have found that gathering together as a committee on a regular basis is very supportive and even necessary for the members. We meet once each month, and it is a time to handle committee business and "housekeeping" details, but it is also a time to share experiences and challenges, to pray with and for each other, to raise questions and concerns, and to learn from each other about different ways of addressing and responding to particular situations.

One of the ground rules for these meetings is that all discussions must remain confidential and not be shared outside the meeting room. We are serving people who at this particular time in their lives are highly vulnerable, and we often hear personal details from the bereaved who trust us and share with us. So I encourage all volunteers to honor this request for privacy.

Often what a volunteer needs most is just the encouragement and reassurance that comes with discovering that others in the ministry are encountering similar stories, feelings and experiences with the grieving. Sometimes a member of the ministry committee simply needs to "check out" what she said during a particular telephone call. Was this okay? What else might I have suggested or said? Most members of the committee at St. Elizabeth have had little contact with persons grieving the loss of a loved one, other than within their own families. So this is new ground for them, and it comes with some level of uncertainty and insecurity. On the other hand, it is also true that they carry with them the realization that their comments and responses to their own family and friends in times of loss is *exactly* what will work as they encounter clients they do not know personally. There is a degree of universality to the compassion that is needed by the bereaved.

Often the entire committee is given a boost by the sharing of a card or note from a client, or a story of thanks and appreciation. It makes all the work worth all the effort. It feels good to hear that our support and presence are making a difference. It is rewarding to hear positive feedback, especially when the ministry is new and just getting off the ground in the parish. One volunteer reported, "This Christmas after I sent the cards to my people, I received a card from one of the first people I had been in contact with saying how much she appreciated our prayers and support. What a great Christmas gift!"

We have also been intentional about including prayer as a priority in our ministry as a committee. I have emphasized, as the leader, that offering sincere prayers for the grieving is not a small gift at all, and prayer offered on behalf of the parish community and priests does hold its own special power. We also pray for each other, for the work that we do, and for God's guidance in our encounters. Each meeting we hold begins and ends with prayer—for those we serve, for those who have died, and for each other and our particular needs and concerns. It bonds us together as a group, and prayer provides a strong foundation for our work together.

Early on in our parish ministry, there was a public commissioning of the committee by our priests at a Sunday Mass, thus establishing us as an official ministry at St. Elizabeth Church. Not only did this ceremony strengthen us as volunteer ministers as we were sent forth to do our work, but it also served to "spotlight" us before the parish community, raising their awareness of our presence and service among them.

The ongoing support of the priests has been both necessary and uplifting for us. Surely any volunteers want and deserve to hear and feel that their efforts are appreciated. But certainly in this difficult work of bereavement, where many shy away from involvement, it is even more essential. While the priests are not needed in order for the actual work to be done, their presence behind the scenes and their acknowledgment serve to encourage and affirm what the volunteers are about. At St. E's we've been blessed with two priests who are deeply interested in the success of this ministry, who are immensely grateful for the benefit to the parish, and who are constantly available to assist in getting the ministry well established in the parish community. This is a tremendous affirmation for me as the one who initiated the effort and now coordinates the group. And it also gives necessary credibility to the volunteers who serve.

Enriching and Educating

One dimension that we are particularly looking at right now for the bereavement ministry group is that of continuing enrichment education and training for the volunteers. To their credit, the volunteers are recognizing this need and requesting ongoing training programs. As coordinator, I believe it is quite important to provide appropriate and informative presentations and/or workshops in order to build confidence and capability in the committee members. If, as we hope, the committee members remain active for an extended period of time, they will share an information base, and we can then build on that, providing more varied and in-depth training as time passes. Also, this desire to gather together for learning seems to indicate growth and stability within the group of volunteers. It is a hopeful sign for the future of the ministry in the parish.

Throughout the first year of our work in the parish, much of our time was spent simply working out the basics of our program. We had to recruit members—

and we continue to recruit because of the large number of funerals in the parish. We compiled and printed a brochure that is sent to all clients offering our services and providing a list of some of the available community resources for grief support, as well as a list of appropriate reading material and websites for those seeking grief support options. We held our initial series of basic training/orientation sessions and held one follow up session about six months later. Some of us attended a workshop on developing parish-based ministries and providing grief support in a parish.

Now that we are established and have moved through our first calendar year, we are planning more specific presentations. For instance, the volunteers are especially interested in learning more about meeting the needs of parents who lose a child. This is a place where we can begin our focused learning. The volunteers recognize that the grief of a parent who has lost a child is a "different" grief that should be addressed in a unique way. At this point most of them are a bit hesitant to minister to a bereaved parent.

This issue of complicated grief situations is significant and does require some attention in the ministry. The coordinator of any bereavement ministry is wise to pay attention to the comfort level of the individual volunteers in dealing with grief. The volunteer ministers need to feel confident and secure as they approach a grieving parishioner to offer support. Sensitivity to the background and experience of the ministers will result in more effective ministry to the grieving. As time passes and the volunteers gain experience and have the opportunities to participate in personal and group education events, the benefits will come in the quality of grief support offered and in the depth of individual personal gratification from the volunteer work.

I continue to make suggestions regarding reading material, to encourage discussion and questions at meetings, and to provide some specific handouts from time to time both for the benefit of the volunteers and to pass along to clients as warranted. I believe our learning needs to be an ongoing process and should increase gradually in depth so that the varied needs of the volunteers are considered and met.

One volunteer at St. Elizabeth's is particularly brave, and I share Sharon's story here to illustrate the beauty of God's presence in our midst. We have been reminded that we are not in charge of how things will unfold; the Holy Spirit is at work, and we are called to listen and follow. Sharon lost a son about a year before joining the bereavement ministry committee. When she was invited to join the group, it was suggested that it might help her with her own grieving process. After prayerful consideration, she agreed to "give it a try." Sharon writes, "Sometimes the work is very hard for me to do. But after talking to the clients and sending cards, it makes me feel very helpful, but also reminds me that there are other people out there hurting also." Sharon continues to work with us, and she continues to process her own grief. About a month after she joined us her mother died, and she is now one of our clients as well as a volunteer. She serves and she is served. Isn't this just what we are called to do as followers of Christ? We serve others as Jesus served us; we allow others to continue to serve us. It is the cycle of Christian discipleship.

Gifting and Grace

This ministry to the bereaved is a ministry that gifts the volunteers. Yes, we are providing particular care and support to a unique population in the parish. But we are receiving, as well, when people who are sad and in pain take the risk of sharing with us. Many people we encounter truly open their hearts and souls in our conversations, and these exchanges are always a rich blessing in our lives. I like to think of them as "holy moments." They are indeed treasures.

I am fortunate to have some first-hand comments and input that affirm the blessing of the ministry. At the end of our first calendar year of existence, I distributed an evaluation form to the volunteers in order to do an assessment of our work. The volunteers commented regarding the leadership of the ministry, suggestions and ideas for improvements and additions, and the things they found to be working well. I also solicited comments on the challenges and the joys the volunteers received in this work over the past year. One person writes: "(The work has brought me) joy! Knowing that I share God's love . . . Everything I give comes from God and in return I receive so much."

Those who are serving as bereavement ministers are encountering others in their "season of weeping." In Old Testament Scripture, the Book of Ecclesiastes tells us that there is indeed a season for everything under heaven. There is no question that it is a difficult and sometimes lonely task—being with another in the season of weeping. But this meeting may also be a time of profound grace, both for the bereaved and for the one offering comfort. It is in just such a time that our God is present to us and with us. A time of weakness and vulnerability can be transformed into a time of strength and courage. The moments of sharing enable growth to happen, and thus the grieving process moves forward. Those called to this special ministry are privileged witnesses to the love and steadfastness of our God and to the gift of our faith as Christians.

And what is the promise Jesus hands down in his teaching on the mountain? In the Gospel of Matthew, we read: "Blessed are they who mourn, for they shall be comforted." The reality is that at some time in our lives each of us will experience a "season of weeping"—probably many such seasons. Not one of us is immune to loss. We trust that indeed we will be comforted by our loving God, and sometimes that comfort will be manifested in the presence of another who cares enough to listen to our story.

QUESTIONS FOR REFLECTION/DISCUSSION

1. Reflect on the importance of a rooted spiritual life for the bereavement minister.

2. What are the benefits of receiving feedback from those served by the ministry?

3. Suggest additional ideas for bonding between committee members.

4. Reflect on your understanding of a "holy moment."

Chapter 5

Go Out into the World

FOR many years the American culture seemed to give minimal focus to the grieving process and to those who experienced the loss of a loved one. Today, we acknowledge more fully the dying process and give more focused attention to all the dynamics and emotions that surround death and loss. And now we also recognize that it is healthy—physically, emotionally, and spiritually—for those left behind to feel deeply and to express fully the loss and pain they experience after the death of a loved one.

The old advice of "don't cry; just move on" is not acceptable anymore as an appropriate response. We affirm the needs of the grieving; we consider their feelings normal, and we accept the opportunity for Christian ministry to this unique population in our midst. We are called as disciples of Jesus Christ to tend to those who hurt and to "shepherd" them through their dark time. We have as our model Jesus and the love he poured out for all. We receive this love and then we carry it to others. Bereavement ministry gives us a chance to help bring the pain of others into the light that is God, thus transforming that same pain into acceptance and hope.

Parishes Reach Out

Let's take some time to look at the variety of options for bereavement ministry both on the parish level, and beyond to the broader church. There are already many programs in place and many possibilities and opportunities for serving the bereaved in our parish communities.

Some parishes (perhaps most parishes) choose to focus on care immediately surrounding the time of death and the funeral. Bereavement ministry often involves the participation of volunteers in the actual funeral liturgy planning and in the provision of food and service for after-funeral receptions. Some committees offer house-sitting and child-sitting so the bereaved family can comfortably attend the visitation and funeral. Transportation assistance might be offered. All of these services provide support and attention to the mourners during the time of initial crisis. It is a very necessary and helpful ministry, particularly in a large parish that has frequent funerals. It can ease the burdens of the pastoral staff and involve the parish members in direct care of one another.

For example, Immaculate Heart of Mary Church in Wilmington, Delaware, has a well-established and coordinated committee which ministers to family members immediately after a death. The committee members participate in planning the funeral mass. They serve as lectors and ministers of Communion when needed, act as ushers for the liturgy, and also provide a meal for a reception of guests if the family wishes. It is a wonderful service to the bereaved, one that conveys the love and concern of the parish community and removes the stress of the practical tasks that are part of the occasion.

Some parishes offer condolence calls by members to those who are experiencing a loss. This visitation takes place at the time of death, at the wake and/or at the funeral liturgy itself. It also serves to involve the parish members in caring for each other and reminds the community that we are Church not only as individuals, but all believers together. We are called to be this universal Church for one another. Whether or not you have a large number of family members and friends surrounding you, the presence and prayers of your spiritual community in a time of sorrow is tremendous reassurance that you are lifted up and carried while you are suffering.

Across the country, there are a number of resources and parish ministry programs in place. Some are extensive and really creative, and they are usually tailored to meet specific needs of individual parish communities. They can be developed and expanded according to the financial and human resources available in each particular parish.

The Cathedral of Mary Our Queen in Baltimore, Maryland, has a three-fold bereavement ministry program in place. The "Shepherd Ministry" there revolves around sending out notes and cards for the first calendar year after a death. Each parish family that loses a loved one receives a set of "Shepherd Guides" to help them get through the significant occasions in the first year. Each "guide" includes a comforting message and an appropriate Scripture passage to help ease the pain of living through those first days and months without the loved one's presence.

Part Two of this same program is six weekly sessions held each fall for the newly bereaved. Resource programs from Ave Maria Press and St. Anthony Messenger Press are integrated into the sessions. And finally, Part Three is a monthly follow-up group based on peer ministry. A past participant of the group serves as the facilitator for a sharing experience that incorporates expression of feelings and prayer in a safe and compassionate environment for the grieving.

In Tampa, Florida, The Church of the Incarnation offers bereavement ministry similar to what we are developing at St. Elizabeth's, although on a larger scale. The ministry is provided by a group of parish volunteers and encompasses both immediate and long-term components following a death. The volunteers are available not only to assist the pastoral staff with the wake and funeral arrangements, but also include a card/letter committee, a support group, educational classes, companioning, and some counseling services. It is an enormous undertaking and an outstanding model of parish lay ministry.

These are just a few examples from the many programs that are operating in parishes across the country. There are countless possibilities for this ministry depending on the needs of the individual parish, the resources and creativity available, and the combined interests and effort of the pastoral staff and the parish community.

There already exists an established organization from which any parish bereavement ministry can obtain a wide variety of resources for its volunteers. The National Catholic Ministry to the Bereaved (NCMB) headquartered in Cleveland, Ohio offers training sessions, workshops, a newsletter, listings of books and pamphlets available for purchase, and much more on their website www.griefwork.org.

Anyone can go online today and investigate the website for NCMB, as well as others, which contain parish descriptions of their ministries, other national organizations, publications, workbooks, videos, etc. The information is readily available for anyone interested in learning about loss, grief, and bereavement ministry. There are regularly scheduled training programs in various geographical locations throughout the calendar year with leaders available to assist as new ministries are organized in parish communities.

Following the True Shepherd

We have a history, as Christians, of gathering around the ones among us who are in pain or crisis. This arises partly out of our desire to share the love of God that was bestowed upon us in a time of difficulty. We received this love; we recognize what it is, and we then feel a need to offer it to others. It is an illustration of the marvelous cycle of "giving" that is at the core of being a disciple of Jesus. It is not at all surprising, then, that many of the volunteers who come forward to work in bereavement ministry are those who have suffered loss themselves, who have experienced an outpouring of Christian love and caring, and who then want to extend this same generous Spirit to others in need. What better way than walking with the mourner . . .companioning the bereaved?

Ministry to the grieving can take on many different faces, and it can address various pieces of the process that surround and follow the death of a loved one. Your particular parish, your community, your priests and lay leaders will have ideas about specific needs, about a desired focus, about the gifts and talents that are present within the parish membership, and about the vision of caring for each other as Church. Take all of these ideas to prayer and reflection. Read and research, listen and discuss your vision for your parish membership. Then develop this vision and move forward to incorporate bereavement ministry into the life and work of your parish community.

Support and serve one another in Christian love, and seek always to walk in the footsteps of Jesus, our Shepherd.

QUESTIONS FOR REFLECTION/DISCUSSION

1. What model of bereavement ministry can you visualize working best in your parish?

2. How does the image of God/Jesus as "Shepherd" speak to you?

3. Spend time in prayer and reflection about your personal call as a disciple of Jesus Christ.

APPENDIX

Prayer Service for Bereavement Ministers

Opening—The leader lights a large votive candle in the center of the group, gathered in a circle, to symbolize those being memorialized.

Scripture Reading—The leader reads one of the following Psalms: Ps 27, 42, 63, 84, 103, 116, 130, 143.

Together we pray:

> Holy and Loving God, as we gather as ministers to the grieving, we ask for your special blessing upon us.
>
> Give to us strength and wisdom to do this work to which we have been called. Help us to open our hearts, to be good listeners, to be caring companions, and to be faithful witnesses to the love and compassion modeled by your Son, Jesus.
>
> Touch those whom we serve with your presence and your grace in their loss and sadness, and bring healing to their hearts. Welcome into the shelter of your embrace all their loved ones.
>
> We pray in the name of the Father and of the Son and of the Holy Spirit. Amen.

Gospel Reading—A member of the group reads one of the following Scripture passages: Matthew 11:25-30, Matthew 5:1-12, John 6:51-59, John 11:17-27, John 12:23-28, John 14:1-6.

Ritual—Each volunteer speaks the name and date of death of one whose family is being served by the ministry, lifting these deceased and their loved ones up in prayer. Let this be done slowly and reverently with soft music in the background.

Together we pray:

> God, Our Father, hear these names we say out loud in your presence.
>
> We give thanks for the lives they lived, for the gifts they shared with family and friends, and for the witness they gave to their faith and their Church.
>
> Be with us as we listen to and console the loved ones who mourn for them. Let us learn from the stories and from the examples that are passed on to us from these men and women.
>
> Let your blessing now be upon each of us who serve as bereavement ministers in *(name of parish)* and also on the bereaved who welcome us into their grief journey.

Joining hands close with the Lord's Prayer.

The leader extinguishes the candle and invites the group to share light refreshments.

Additional Resources for Bereavement Ministry

Books and Other Resources

Bozarth-Campbell, Alla. *Life Is Goodbye, Life Is Hello: Grieving Through All Kinds of Loss* (Minneapolis: Compcare, 1982).

CareNote Resources, Abbey Press, One Caring Place, St. Meinrad, Indiana 47577.

Dues, Greg and Walkley, Barbara. *Called To Parish Ministry: Identity, Challenges,* and *Spirituality of Lay Ministers* (Mystic, CT: Twenty Third Publications, 1995).

Kubler-Ross, Elizabeth. *On Death and Dying* (New York: Macmillan, 1969).

Kushner, Harold. *When Bad Things Happen to Good People* (New York: Avon Books, 1981).

Levine, Stephen. *A Year to Live* (New York: Bell Tower, 1997).

Nelson, Jan and Aaker, David. *The Bereavement Ministry Program: A Comprehensive Guide for Churches* (Notre Dame: Ave Maria, 1998).

Rupp, Joyce. *Praying Our Goodbyes* (Notre Dame: Ave Maria, 1988, 1999).

Smith, Keith. *Mourning Sickness* (New Jersey: Resurrection Press, 2003).

Viorst, Judith. *Necessary Losses* (New York: Simon and Schuster, 1986).

Organizations

National Catholic Ministry to the Bereaved
606 Middle Avenue
Elyria, Ohio 44035
(440) 323-6262
www.griefwork.org

Association for Death Education and Counseling
638 Prospect Avenue
Hartford, Connecticut 06105-4298
www.ADEC.org

Diocesan Offices

Local counseling centers and funeral homes

Community Resource Centers for toll-free numbers